D1287339

STATE PROFILES

ALASKA

BY COLLEEN SEXTON

BLASTOFF! DISCOVERY

BELLWETHER MEDIA • MINNEAPOLIS, MN

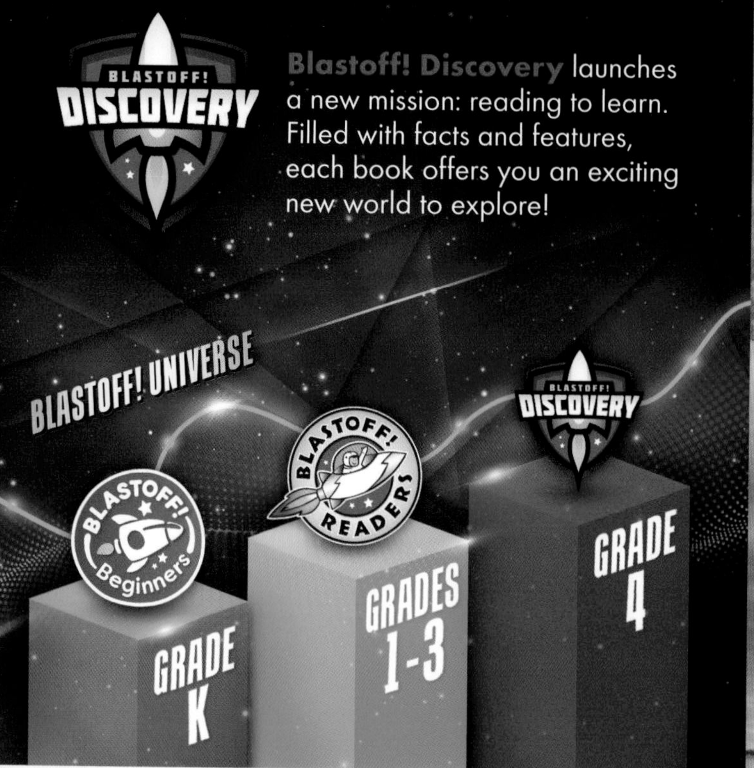

This edition first published in 2022 by Bellwether Media, Inc.

Library of Congress Cataloging-in-Publication Data

Names: Sexton, Colleen A., 1967- author.
Title: Alaska / by Colleen Sexton.
Description: Minneapolis, MN : Bellwether Media, 2022. | Series: Blastoff! Discovery: State profiles | Includes bibliographical references and index. | Audience: Ages 7-13 | Audience: Grades 4-6 | Summary: "Engaging images accompany information about Alaska. The combination of high-interest subject matter and narrative text is intended for students in grades 3 through 8"–Provided by publisher.
Identifiers: LCCN 2021019669 (print) | LCCN 2021019670 (ebook) | ISBN 9781644873731 (library binding) | ISBN 9781648341502 (ebook)
Subjects: LCSH: Alaska–Juvenile literature.
Classification: LCC F904.3 .S49 2022 (print) | LCC F904.3 (ebook) | DDC 979.8–dc23
LC record available at https://lccn.loc.gov/2021019669
LC ebook record available at https://lccn.loc.gov/2021019670

Editor: Kate Moening   Designer: Brittany McIntosh

Printed in the United States of America, North Mankato, MN.

TABLE OF CONTENTS

KENAI FJORDS NATIONAL PARK

A tour boat leaves the dock in Kenai Fjords National Park. The passengers are ready for adventure! The captain steers along the coast. Rocky shores rise into mountains. Narrow waterfalls tumble down cliffs. Puffins nest in the cliff walls.

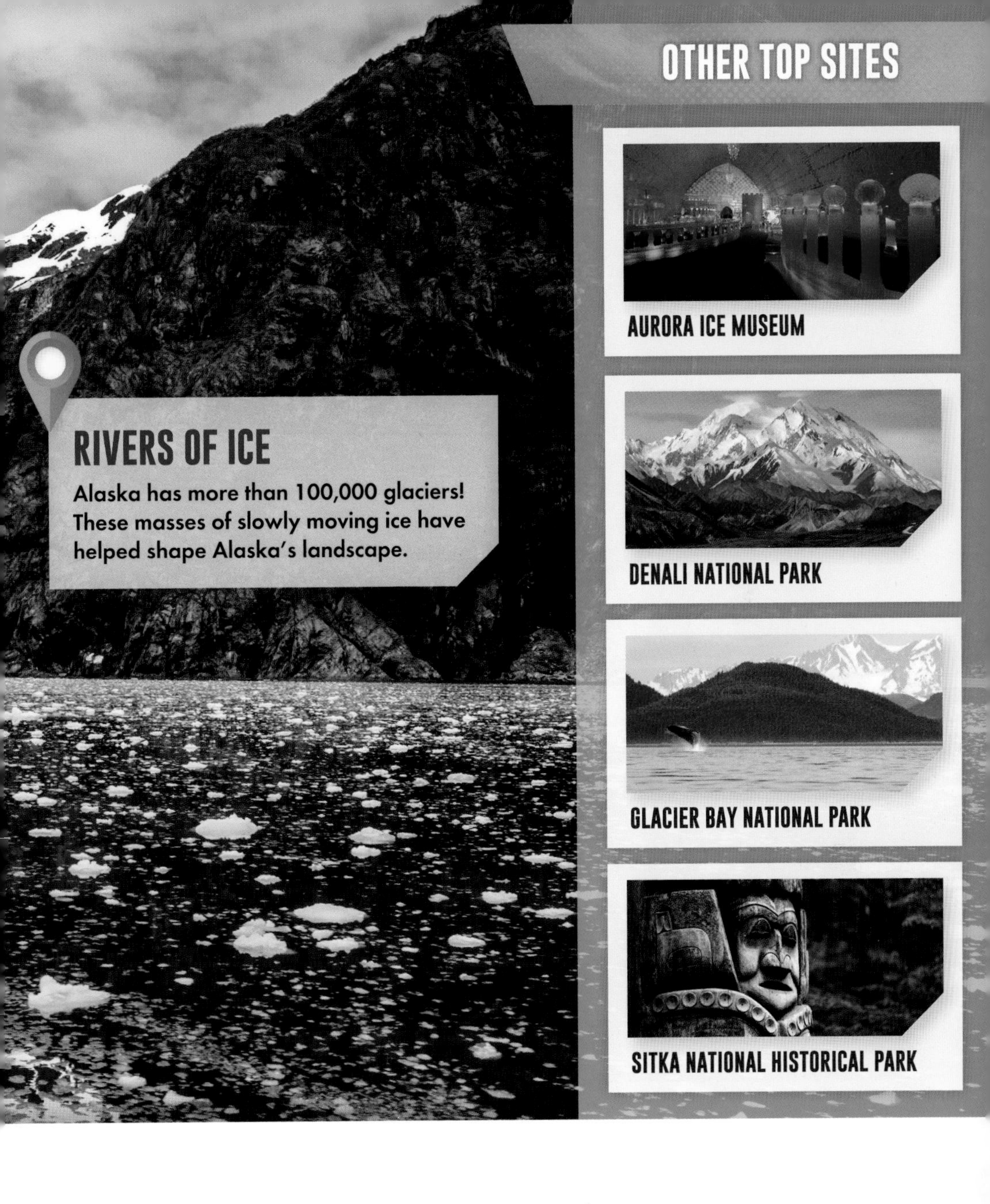

The boat passes by **icebergs** and approaches the Harding Icefield. CRACK! A huge chunk of ice falls from a **glacier** into the ocean. The boat heads back to the dock. Along the way, passengers spy playful otters and harbor seals. They even see a humpback whale come up for air. Welcome to Alaska!

Alaska is the largest state. This huge **peninsula** covers 665,384 square miles (1,723,337 square kilometers). It shares its only land border with Canada to the east. The Alaska Highway crosses this border and connects Alaska to the lower 48 states.

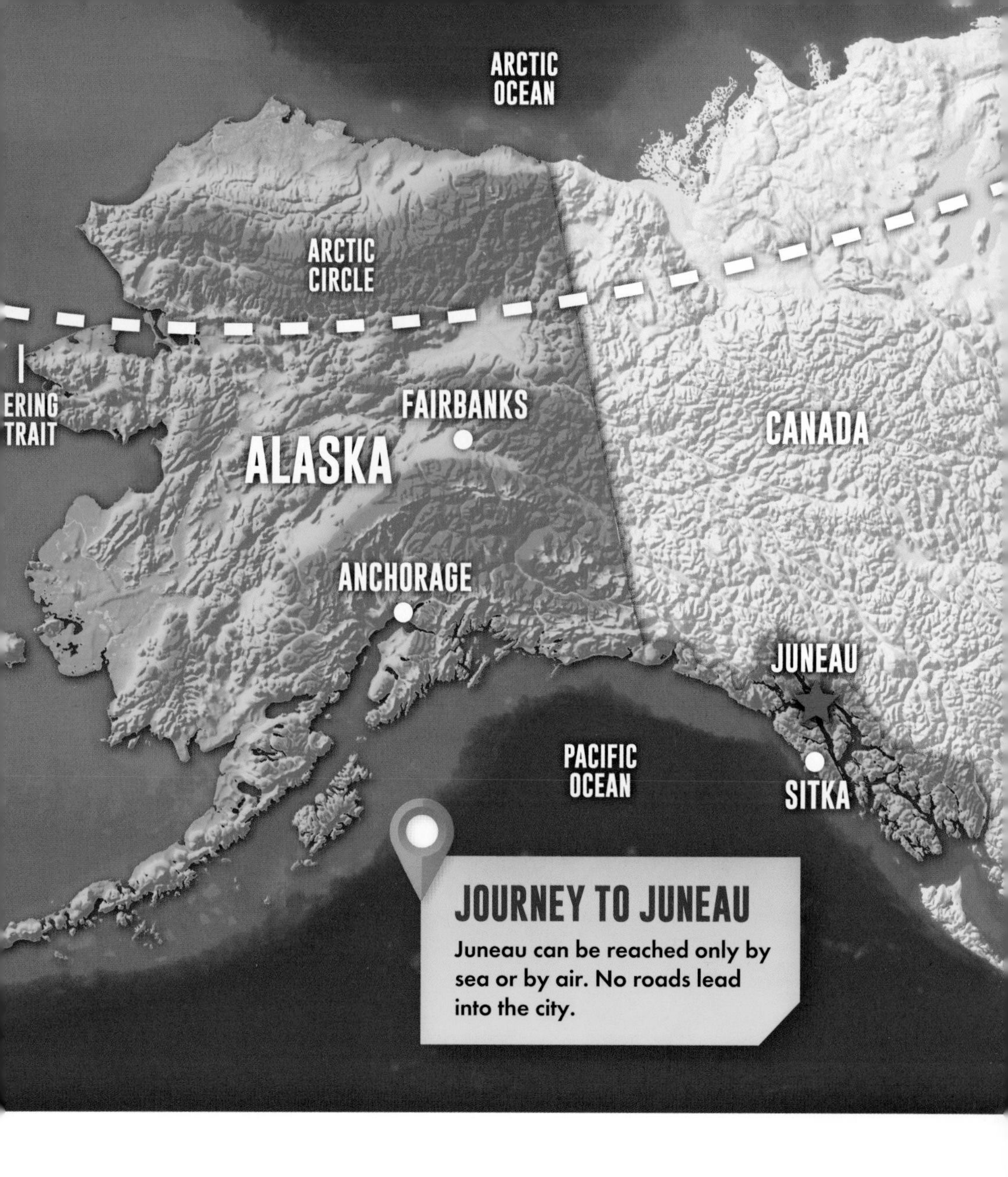

Alaska lies farther north and west than any other state. One-third of Alaska reaches above the **Arctic Circle**. Its northern coast meets the Arctic Ocean. Russia lies 55 miles (89 kilometers) to the west, across the Bering **Strait**. The Bering Sea borders southwestern Alaska. The Pacific Ocean washes upon the state's southern border. Alaska's capital, Juneau, sits on the southeastern coast.

ALASKA'S BEGINNINGS

TLINGIT PEOPLE

The first people arrived in Alaska from Russia at least 15,000 years ago. These peoples were **ancestors** of **Alaska Natives**. Later, the Inuit and Yupik fished and hunted in coastal areas. The Athabascans followed herds of caribou inland. The Aleuts hunted sea animals for food and clothing. The Tlingit, Haida, and Tsimshian became artists and warriors.

In 1741, explorer Vitus Bering claimed Alaska for Russia. Russian fur traders soon moved into the area. In 1867, the United States purchased Alaska from Russia. The discovery of gold brought miners to the region in the late 1800s. Alaska became the 49th state in 1959.

NATIVE PEOPLES OF ALASKA

YUPIK

- **Original lands in western and southwestern Alaska**
- **Around 34,000 live in Alaska today**

INUIT

- **Original lands on the far northern and western coasts of Alaska**
- **Around 33,000 live in Alaska today**
- **Also called Iñupiat**

ATHABASCAN

- **Original lands were hunting grounds in inland Alaska**
- **Around 22,000 live in Alaska today**

TLINGIT, HAIDA, AND TSIMSHIAN

- **Original lands along Alaska's southeastern coast**
- **Around 30,000 live in Alaska today**
- **Haida also called Kaigani**

ALEUT

- **Original lands on the Aleutian Islands**
- **Around 19,000 live in Alaska today**
- **Also called Sugpiaq and Unangax**

LANDSCAPE AND CLIMATE

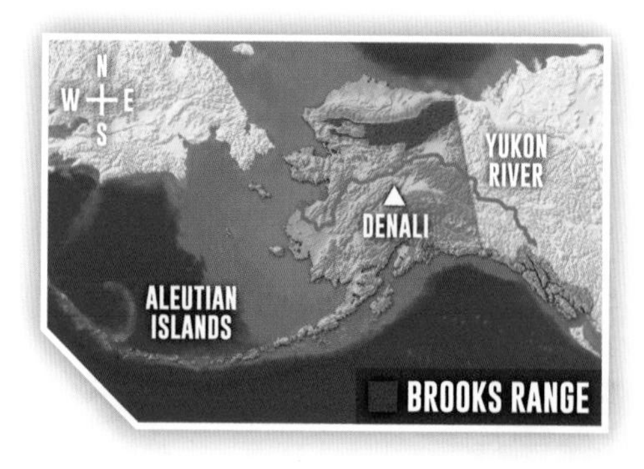

Tundra covers northern Alaska. The Brooks Range rises south of this frozen plain. Hills and lakes cover central Alaska. There, the Yukon River flows west through thick forests. To the south, glaciers fill the valleys of the Alaska Range. This huge mountain range features Denali, the highest peak in North America. The rocky Aleutian Islands arc southwest across the Bering Sea. A **temperate rain forest** grows on Alaska's southeastern coast.

YUKON RIVER

IN THE DARK

Alaskans experience the midnight sun in summer and polar night in winter. In the northernmost city of Utqiagvik, the sun does not set for around 84 days in the summer. There is no daylight for around 64 days in winter.

DENALI
ALASKA RANGE

SEASONAL HIGHS AND LOWS

SPRING
HIGH: 31°F (-1°C)
LOW: 3°F (-16°C)

SUMMER
HIGH: 64°F (18°C)
LOW: 43°F (6°C)

FALL
HIGH: 21°F (-6°C)
LOW: 1°F (-17°C)

WINTER
HIGH: -7°F (-22°C)
LOW: -28°F (-33°C)

°F = degrees Fahrenheit
°C = degrees Celsius

Summer in Alaska ranges from cool in the north to mild in the south. Winter brings heavy snow and below-freezing temperatures to much of the state.

WILDLIFE

Alaska is famous for its wildlife. Seals and walruses relax on the Arctic ice where polar bears prowl. Large herds of caribou feed on the tundra. Musk oxen wander grasslands in western and northern Alaska. Brown bears, moose, and wolves roam the state's forests. Mountain goats and Dall sheep climb rough peaks. Foxes, minks, and martens brave Alaska's cold winters with thick fur coats.

Eagles, hawks, and ospreys swoop across Alaska's skies in search of prey. Salmon and halibut swim off the coast, where gulls dive for fish. Albatrosses search for squids farther out. Alaska's ocean waters are also home to humpback whales, orcas, and gray whales.

MUSK OX

DALL SHEEP

SOCKEYE SALMON

ORCA

ALBATROSS

ALASKA'S FUTURE: CATCHING FIRE

Climate change is bringing warmer and drier conditions to Alaska. These changes have led to more wildfires. The fires change animals' habitats and affect their food supply.

POLAR BEAR

Life Span: about 25 years
Status: vulnerable

polar bear range =

LEAST CONCERN	NEAR THREATENED	VULNERABLE	ENDANGERED	CRITICALLY ENDANGERED	EXTINCT IN THE WILD	EXTINCT
		▲				

PEOPLE AND COMMUNITIES

Alaska is known as America's Last **Frontier** because much of the state is still unsettled wilderness. About 700,000 people live in Alaska. Most live in Anchorage, Juneau, and Fairbanks. About one in three Alaskans live in small communities along coasts, highways, and rivers.

SKAGWAY

FAMOUS ALASKAN

Name: Susan Butcher

Born: December 26, 1954

Died: August 5, 2006

Hometown: Eureka, Alaska

Famous For: Though not born in Alaska, this famed musher won the Iditarod Trail Sled Dog Race four times, is the only musher to win the race three times in a row, and is now honored in the state in March each year for Susan Butcher Day

Most Alaskans have ancestors from Europe. Alaska Natives and Native Americans make up the next-largest group. Many Haida, Tlingit, and Tsimshian people live in the Metlakatla Indian Community in the southeast. Other Alaska Natives live on their **traditional** lands. Recent **immigrants** have come from Mexico, Korea, the Philippines, and Thailand. Some residents have moved to Alaska from other states.

SPECIAL DELIVERY

Alaska's bush pilots crisscross the state in their small planes. People in distant locations depend on these pilots for transportation and supplies.

ANCHORAGE

Founded in 1914, Anchorage is Alaska's largest city. It was named because ships anchored there to deliver railroad supplies. Today, Anchorage is home to about half of the state's population. It is a **tourist** destination, a chief port, and a center for shipping freight by air to Asia. A large U.S. military base lies just north of the city.

Anchorage offers a variety of experiences. Exhibits at the Anchorage Museum and the Alaska Native **Heritage** Center explore Alaska's story. Audiences applaud the Anchorage Symphony Orchestra and the Anchorage Opera. Residents enjoy the city's network of bike and ski trails year-round.

INDUSTRY

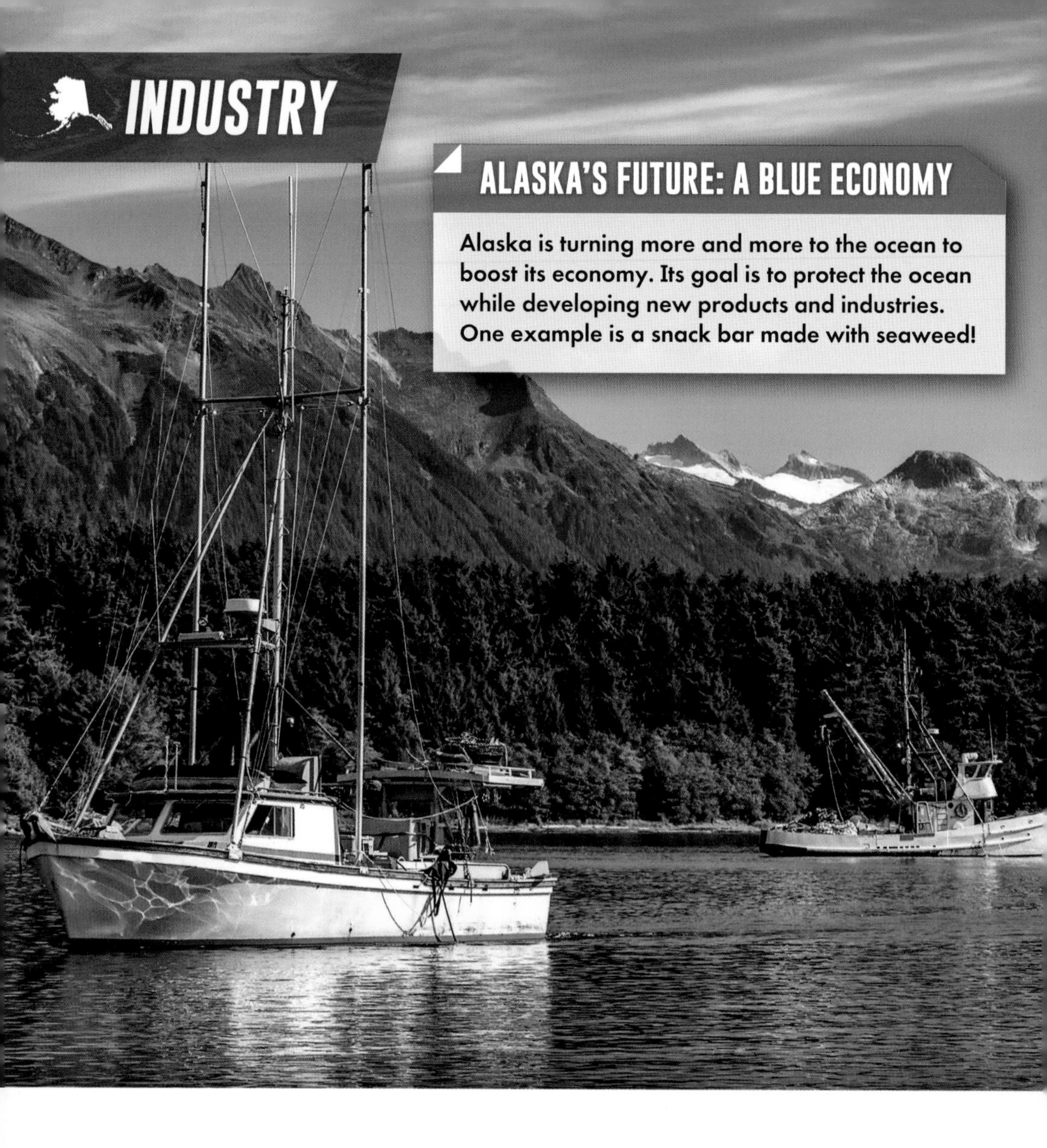

ALASKA'S FUTURE: A BLUE ECONOMY

Alaska is turning more and more to the ocean to boost its economy. Its goal is to protect the ocean while developing new products and industries. One example is a snack bar made with seaweed!

Natural resources have drawn people to Alaska since the discovery of gold in the late 1800s. Today, workers still mine gold, as well as silver and zinc. The biggest mining business is oil. The Trans-Alaska Pipeline carries oil south from northern Alaska. Ships transport the oil to other states. On coastal waters, fishing boats haul in salmon, halibut, and crab. Most seafood is shipped out of state.

Most Alaskans have **service jobs**. They work in health care, construction, and transportation. Tourism employs hotel workers, restaurant servers, and tour guides. Some service workers find jobs on cruise ships or in Alaska's many national parks.

FOOD

GRILLED SALMON

Alaska's coastal waters offer plentiful seafood. Salmon is popular. Cooks serve it grilled, baked, poached, and smoked. Diners also enjoy fresh crab, shrimp, and scallops. Leftover seafood is often made into chowders and stews.

A HUGE HARVEST

Alaska's long summer days often produce oversized fruits and vegetables. Gardeners have famously harvested a 35-pound (16-kilogram) broccoli, a 65-pound (29-kilogram) cantaloupe, and a 138-pound (63-kilogram) cabbage!

Many Alaska Natives continue their tradition of hunting seals, whales, and walruses for food. Some raise herds of reindeer for meat. Reindeer dogs are a popular street food. These hot dogs are topped with mustard, cream cheese, and onions cooked with Coca-Cola. In many parts of the state, Alaskans harvest wild blueberries, raspberries, and cloudberries. Berries are common in the traditional dessert *akutaq*.

SEAFOOD CHOWDER

REINDEER DOG

AKUTAQ

5 SERVINGS

Have an adult help you make this frozen treat!

INGREDIENTS

- 1 cup shortening
- 1 cup sugar
- 1/2 cup water
- 4 cups berries

DIRECTIONS

1. Cut up the shortening and add it to a pot. Stir slowly over low heat until it is melted.
2. Stir in the sugar until it is dissolved.
3. Remove from heat when the whole mixture is liquid. Stir in 1/4 cup of water.
4. Stir until the mixture has cooled and thickened.
5. Add the rest of the water.
6. When the mixture is fluffy, add the berries.
7. Freeze for at least 1 hour. Enjoy!

IDITAROD TRAIL SLED DOG RACE

Dog **mushing** is Alaska's state sport. The biggest race is the Iditarod Trail Sled Dog Race in March. Teams cover 1,100 miles (1,770 kilometers) of snow and ice. The trail from Anchorage to Nome usually takes about 10 to 14 days to complete.

HITCHING A RIDE

Skijoring is a popular winter sport in Alaska. Skiers hitch themselves to dogs that pull them through the snow.

Alaska's parks draw hikers, campers, and climbers. Kayakers brave rushing rivers and ocean waters. Snowmobilers and skiers enjoy winter snow. Bird-watching is popular year-round. Residents tour Alaska's many museums to learn about state history. Photographers try to capture the **northern lights**. Some Alaskans pan for gold as a hobby. Alaska Natives may practice basketry, wood carving, beadwork, and other traditional arts.

NOTABLE SPORTS TEAM

Alaska Nanooks, University of Alaska Fairbanks
Sport: Western Collegiate Hockey Association
Started: 1925
Place of Play: Carlson Center in Fairbanks

FESTIVALS AND TRADITIONS

Alaskans enjoy many seasonal festivals. People bundle up for winter's Fur Rondy in Anchorage. They enjoy snowshoe softball games and outhouse races. Every February and March, sculptors compete in the World Ice Art Championship in Fairbanks. Sculptures light up at night for huge crowds.

Every summer, native peoples gather in Fairbanks for the World Eskimo-Indian Olympics. Athletes show off in traditional events like the blanket toss and the four-man carry. The state's largest event is the Alaska State Fair in late August. Summer also brings the longest day of the year. Some Alaskans take midnight hikes to celebrate the Land of the Midnight Sun!

WORLD ICE ART CHAMPIONSHIP

Tyvek
HomeWrap
The miracles of science
Tyvek
HomeWrap
DUPONT

ALASKA TIMELINE

1741

Vitus Bering explores Alaska and claims it for Russia

1867

The United States purchases Alaska from Russia for $7.2 million

1906

Juneau becomes Alaska's capital

1959

Alaska becomes the 49th state

1964

A powerful 9.2 magnitude earthquake strikes Alaska

1968

The largest oil field in North America is discovered in northern Alaska's Prudhoe Bay

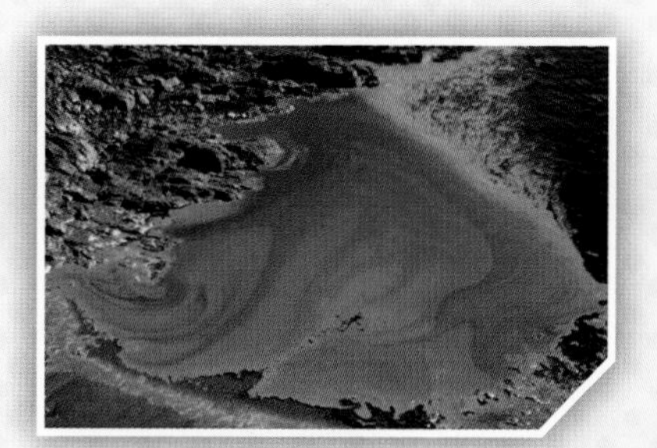

1971

The Alaska Native Claims Settlement Act gives $962.5 million and about 44 million acres (17.8 million hectares) of land to the state's native peoples

1989

The Exxon Valdez ship spills 11 million gallons (41.6 million liters) of oil off Alaska's southern coast

2017

After decades of legal battles, a law passes to allow oil drilling in the Arctic National Wildlife Refuge

1975–77

The Trans-Alaska Pipeline is built between Prudhoe Bay in the north and Valdez in the south

ALASKA FACTS

Nicknames: The Last Frontier, The Great Land, Land of the Midnight Sun

Motto: North to the Future

Date of Statehood: January 3, 1959 (the 49th state)

Capital City: Juneau ★

Other Major Cities: Anchorage, Fairbanks, Sitka

Area: 665,384 square miles (1,723,337 square kilometers); Alaska is the largest state.

STATE FLAG

Alaska's state flag has a dark blue background. Blue represents Alaska's sky and the wildflowers that grow in the state. The stars of the Big Dipper, or Great Bear, are on the left. They stand for strength. The North Star on the right shows that Alaska is the northernmost state. It also represents the state's future.

INDUSTRY

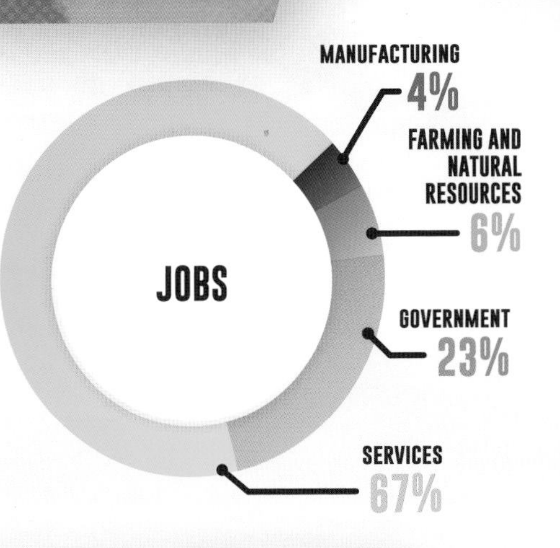

Main Exports

oil | natural gas | seafood

gold | lead | zinc

Natural Resources

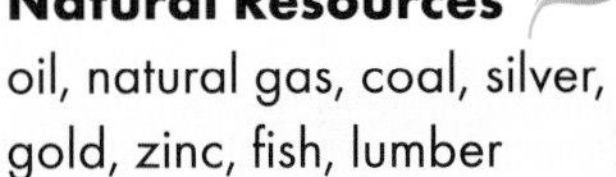

oil, natural gas, coal, silver, gold, zinc, fish, lumber

GOVERNMENT

3 ELECTORAL VOTES

Federal Government

1 REPRESENTATIVE | 2 SENATORS

USA

State Government

40 REPRESENTATIVES | 20 SENATORS

STATE SYMBOLS

STATE BIRD
WILLOW PTARMIGAN

STATE FISH
KING SALMON

STATE FLOWER
ALPINE FORGET-ME-NOT

STATE TREE
SITKA SPRUCE

GLOSSARY

Alaska Natives—any of the original people groups that lived in Alaska before European settlers arrived; they include Aluets, Yupik, Inuit, Athabascans, Tlingit, Haida, and Tsimshian.

ancestors—relatives who lived long ago

Arctic Circle—an imaginary line that circles the top of the globe, parallel to the equator

frontier—the edge of a settled land

glacier—a massive sheet of ice that covers a large area of land

heritage—the traditions, achievements, and beliefs that are part of the history of a group of people

icebergs—large, floating masses of ice that have broken off from glaciers

immigrants—people who move to a new country

mushing—a sport in which a person rides on a sled behind a team of dogs

natural resources—materials in the earth that are taken out and used to make products or fuel

northern lights—bands of light also called the aurora borealis that appear in the night sky in northern regions

peninsula—a section of land that extends out from a larger piece of land and is almost completely surrounded by water

service jobs—jobs that perform tasks for people or businesses

strait—a narrow channel connecting two large bodies of water

temperate rain forest—a thick, green forest that has mild temperatures and receives a lot of rain

tourist—related to the business of people traveling to visit other places

traditional—related to customs, ideas, or beliefs handed down from one generation to the next

tundra—treeless land that is permanently frozen beneath the surface

TO LEARN MORE

AT THE LIBRARY

Gregory, Josh. *Alaska*. New York, N.Y.: Children's Press, 2018.

Peratrovich, Roy A. *Little Whale: A Story of the Last Tlingit War Canoe*. Fairbanks, Alas.: University of Alaska Press, 2016.

Viola, Jason. *Polar Bears: Survival on the Ice*. New York, N.Y.: First Second, 2019.

ON THE WEB

FACTSURFER

Factsurfer.com gives you a safe, fun way to find more information.

1. Go to www.factsurfer.com.
2. Enter "Alaska" into the search box and click 🔍.
3. Select your book cover to see a list of related content.

INDEX

The images in this book are reproduced through the courtesy of: Feng Yu, front cover, pp. 2-3; ILYA AKINSHIN, p. 3; A&J Fotos/ Getty Images, pp. 4-5; Reimar, p. 5 (Aurora Ice Museum); Steve Allen, p. 5 (Denali); TyMaloney, p. 5 (Glacier Bay); Brad Mitchell/ Alamy, p. 5 (Sitka National Historical Park); National Geographic Image Collection/ Alamy, p. 8; Matej Halouska, p. 9; Patrick J. Endres/ Getty Images, p. 10; Real Window Creative, p. 11 (top); valiant.skies, p. 11 (bottom); Anton Rodionov, p. 12 (albatross); Martin Hejzlar, p. 12 (musk ox); Patrick Lynch Photography, p. 12 (Dall sheep); Vasik Olga, p. 12 (sockeye salmon); Christian Musat, p. 12 (orca); chbaum, p. 13; Darryl Brooks, p. 14; Kirk Geisler, p. 15 (top); Design Pics Inc/ Alamy, pp. 15 (middle), 17, 20 (bottom); joeborg, p. 15 (bottom); Russ Heinl, p. 16; SeregaSibTravel, p. 18; Hurst Photo, p. 19 (ranch dressing); Chiyacat, p. 19 (ulu); marekuliasz, p. 19 (kayak); MaxFX, p. 19 (bottom); W. Scott McGill, p. 20 (top); Foodio, p. 21 (chowder); Travis S./ Flickr, p. 21 (reindeer dog); Matyáš Havel/ Wikipedia, p. 21 (akutaq); grey_and, p. 21 (blueberries); Troutnut, p. 22 (top); ZUMA Press Inc/ Alamy, pp. 22 (bottom), 23 (middle); Gail Johnson, p. 23 (top); aperturesound, p. 23 (bottom); Gary Whitton, p. 24; Loren Holmes/ Alamy, pp. 24-25; Институт Археологии РАН/ Wikipedia, p. 26 (top); Millennium, p. 26 (bottom); Accent Alaska.com/ Alamy, p. 27 (top); Heather Lucia Snow, p. 27 (bottom); V. Belov, p. 29 (willow ptarmigan); Kevin Cass, p. 29 (king salmon); Gherzak, p. 29 (forget-me-not); Tim Hancock, p. 29 (Sitka spruce); Holy Polygon, p. 31.